Bluebeard

A MELODRAMA IN THREE ACTS

By Charles Ludlam

No part of this book may be reproduced, stored in a retrieval system, or transmitted in any form, by any means, including mechanical, electronic, photocopying, recording, or otherwise, without the prior written permission of the publisher.

SAMUEL FRENCH, INC.
45 WEST 25TH STREET   NEW YORK 10010
7623 SUNSET BOULEVARD   HOLLYWOOD 90046
LONDON   *TORONTO*

Copyright ©, 1971, by Charles Ludlam
Copyright ©, 1987, by The Estate of Charles Ludlam
ALL RIGHTS RESERVED

CAUTION: Professionals and amateurs are hereby warned that BLUEBEARD is subject to a royalty. It is fully protected under the copyright laws of the United States of America, the British Commonwealth, including Canada, and all other countries of the Copyright Union. All rights, including professional, amateur, motion pictures, recitation, lecturing, public reading, radio broadcasting, television, and the rights of translation into foreign languages are strictly reserved. In its present form the play is dedicated to the reading public only.

BLUEBEARD may be given stage presentation by amateurs upon payment of a royalty of Sixty Dollars for the first performance, and Forty Dollars for each additional performance, payable one week before the date when the play is given to Samuel French, Inc., at 45 West 25th Street, New York, N.Y. 10010, or at 7623 Sunset Boulevard, Hollywood, Calif. 90046, or to Samuel French (Canada), Ltd., 80 Richmond Street East, Toronto, Ontario, Canada M5C 1P1.

Royalty of the required amount must be paid whether the play is presented for charity or gain and whether or not admission is charged.

Stock royalty quoted on application to Samuel French, Inc.

For all other rights than those stipulated above, apply to Samuel French, Inc. 45 West 25th Street, New York, N.Y. 10010.

Particular emphasis is laid on the question of amateur or professional readings, permission and terms for which must be secured in writing from Samuel French, Inc.

Copying from this book in whole or in part is strictly forbidden by law, and the right of performance is not transferable.

Whenever the play is produced the following notice must appear on all programs, printing and advertising for the play: "Produced by special arrangement with Samuel French, Inc."

Due authorship credit must be given on all programs, printing and advertising for the play.

> Anyone presenting the play shall not commit or authorize any act or omission by which the copyright of the play or the right to copyright same may be impaired.

> No changes shall be made in the play for the purpose of your production unless authorized in writing.

> The publication of this play does not imply that it is necessarily available for performance by amateurs or professionals. Amateurs and professionals considering a production are strongly advised in their own interests to apply to Samuel French, Inc., for consent before starting rehearsals, advertising, or booking a theatre or hall.

Printed in U.S.A.
ISBN 0 573 69071 5

BILLING AND CREDIT REQUIREMENTS

All producers of BLUEBEARD must give credit to the Author in all programs and in all instances in which the title of the Play appears for purposes of advertising, publicizing or otherwise exploiting the Play and/or production. The author's name must appear on a separate line in which no other name appears, immediately following the title of the play, and must appear in size of type not less than fifty percent the size of title type.

Bluebeard was first presented by The Ridiculous Theatrical Company at La Mama ETC, New York City, on March 26, 1970, with the following cast:

SHEEMISH	*John Brockmeyer*
MRS. MAGGOT	*Eleven*
KHANAZAR VON BLUEBEARD	*Charles Ludlam*
GOOD ANGEL	*James Morfogen*
BAD ANGEL	*Fredrick "Dude" Teper*
SYBIL	*Black-Eyed Susan*
RODNEY	*Bill Vehr*
MISS CUBBIDGE	*Lola Pashalinski*
LAMIA "THE LEOPARD WOMAN"	*Mario Montez*
HECATE	*Lohr Wilson*
HER TRAIN	*James Morfogen, Fredrick "Dude" Teper*

It was directed by the author. Settings by Christopher Scott and Sam Yahn; lighting by Leandro Katz; costumes by Mary Brecht. Music and sound by David Scott.

Bluebeard

ACT ONE:
THE EAVESDROPPER

Scene: The alchemical laboratory of Dr. Bluebeard, located on an island off the coast of Maine. The house is a lighthouse still in use. Revolving light, test tubes and other laboratory equipment including an operating table. SHEEMISH, the butler, and MRS. MAGGOT, the housekeeper, are dusting and sweeping. MRS. MAGGOT bumps the table, causing a test tube to fall and break.

Scene 1
SHEEMISH, MRS. MAGGOT

SHEEMISH. Now see what you've done! Clean it up at once. For if Khanazar, the Bluebeard, finds anything broken, he will surely send you to the House of Pain.

MRS. MAGGOT. (*terribly frightened*) No, no, not the House of Pain!

SHEEMISH. (*sadistically*) Yes, yes, the House of Pain. If I should mention the fact that you broke this little glass tube, I'm sure the master would send you to the House of Pain.

MRS. MAGGOT. (*more frightened*) No, no, not the House of Pain! Please, Sheemish, don't tell, I beg of you.

SHEEMISH. (*calculatingly*) Very well. I will not tell . . . as long as you realize that I am doing you a favor . . . and that I will expect a favor in return.

MRS. MAGGOT. Anything, I'll do anything you ask, but please, please do not tell.

SHEEMISH. Replace the little glass tube. Substitute something for the sticky liquid inside. Do this quickly, for the good ship *Lady Vain* will dock here at three o'clock this afternoon, drop off a female passenger and return to the mainland. We must prepare the guest room for tonight . . . and the bridal chamber for tomorrow.

MRS. MAGGOT. You mean he's found another, another (*She begins to weep.*) . . . ?

SHEEMISH. Say it, Mrs. Maggot! Wife. Say it: Wife! Wife! Wife!

MRS. MAGGOT. I can't. I can't bear to say it. (*falling to her knees*) Lord of my prayers! God of my sacrifice! Because you have done this thing, you shall lack both my fear and my praise. I shall not wince at your lightnings nor be awed when you go by.

SHEEMISH. Curse not our god, Khanazar, the Bluebeard.

MRS. MAGGOT. Why should I not curse him who has stolen from me the gardens of my childhood?

SHEEMISH. Remember the House of Pain and hold your tongue. You have replaced the little glass tube. It looks exactly as it did before the little accident. Even the liquid is the same color and viscosity. You and I are the only ones who know. Come, the guest room. And, Mrs. Maggot, forget about the past.

MRS. MAGGOT. Since the operation I can't remember it anyway.

SHEEMISH. And think as I do, of the future.

MRS. MAGGOT.
The future is so very far.
The present is what must be feared.

For we are slaves of Khanazar,
And dread the wrath of the Bluebeard.

Scene 2
LAMIA THE LEOPARD WOMAN

Enter LAMIA THE LEOPARD WOMAN, wearing more leopard than the costume designer thought advisable.

Scene 3
KHANAZAR THE BLUEBEARD

BLUEBEARD. (*entering and seeing LAMIA*) I thought I told you never to come to this side of the island again? (*Draws gun and fires. Lamia runs out.*) Give up your passions, Bluebeard, and become the thing you claim to be. Is to end desire desire's chiefest end? Does sex afford no greater miracles? Have all my perversions and monstrosities, my fuckings and suckings led me to this? This little death at the climax followed by slumber? Yet chastity ravishes me. And yet the cunt gapes like the jaws of hell, an unfathomable abyss; or the boy-ass used to buggery spread wide to swallow me up its bung; or the mouth sucking out my life! Aaagh! If only there were some new and gentle genital that would combine with me and, mutually interpenetrated, steer me through this storm in paradise! (*the sound of a foghorn*) They said I was mad at medical school. They said no third genital was possible. Yang and yin, male and female and that's that. (*laughs maniacally*) Science suits a mercenary drudge who aims at nothing but external trash. Give me a dark art that stretches as far as does the mind of man; a sound magician is a demigod. (*Foghorn again.*)

SCENE 4
GOOD ANGEL, BAD ANGEL, BLUEBEARD

GOOD ANGEL.
On, Bluebeard, lay these thoughts aside,
And think not on them lest it tempt thy soul
And heap God's heavy wrath upon thee.
Take half — one sex, that's all — for that is nature's way.

(*Foghorn.*)

BAD ANGEL.
Go forward, Bluebeard, in that famous art
Wherein all nature's treasure is contained:
Be thou on earth as God is in the sky,
Master and possessor of both sexes.

(*Exit ANGELS.*)

SCENE 5
BLUEBEARD

BLUEBEARD.
Love must be reinvented, that's obvious.
Sex to me no longer is mysterious
And so I swear that while my beard is blue,
I'll twist some human flesh into a genital new.

Scene 6
BLUEBEARD, SHEEMISH, MRS. MAGGOT

SHEEMISH. Master, Master.

BLUEBEARD. (*enraged*) Swine! How dare you enter my room without knocking? (*lashes whip*) Have you forgotten the House of Pain?

SHEEMISH. (*clutching his genitals*) No, no, not the House of Pain! Mercy, Master.

BLUEBEARD. How can I show you mercy when I am merciless with myself? I see in you nothing but my own failure; another experiment down the drain.

SHEEMISH. (*on his knees pathetically*) Forgive me. (*whimpers*)

BLUEBEARD. Aaagh, get up. Tell me what you want.

SHEEMISH. The good ship *Lady Vain* has docked here on the rocky side of the island.

BLUEBEARD. (*anticipating*) Yes . . .

SHEEMISH. There are two women . . .

BLUEBEARD. (*in ecstasy*) Ah, resolve me of all ambiguities. Perform what desperate enterprises I will!

MRS. MAGGOT. And a man.

BLUEBEARD. Huh? A man? There is no man! (*lashes her with whip*) You are mistaken, there is no man.

(*Loud knocking at the door.*)

MRS. MAGGOT. It's them.

SHEEMISH. (*correcting her*) It is they.

BLUEBEARD. (*looking through spy hole*) Sybil said nothing about a man. (*loud knocking, howling wind and the sound of rain*) Go away! Go away! Leave me in peace!

10 BLUEBEARD

SCENE 7
*BLUEBEARD, SHEEMISH, MRS. MAGGOT,
RODNEY PARKER, SYBIL,
MISS FLORA CUBBIDGE*

RODNEY'S VOICE. Baron Bluebeard, please open the door!
BLUEBEARD. Leave me alone! Go away!
SYBIL'S VOICE. Dear Uncle, please let us in for the love of God. It's bitter without.
BLUEBEARD. (*aside*) And I am bitter within!
MISS CUBBIDGE'S VOICE. We'll catch our death of cold!
MRS. MAGGOT. (*in confusion*) What should we do, Master?
SHEEMISH. (*calling down from a lookout point*) We must let them in for their ship, the *Lady Vain*, its sails big-bellied, makes way from our port. I think it will go down in the storm.
BLUEBEARD. Aagh, very well, come in then. But you can't stay. (*opens the door*)

(*Enter SYBIL, RODNEY and CUBBIDGE, wet.*)

SYBIL. (*rushing to BLUEBEARD*) Oh Uncle Khanazar, my dear Uncle Khanazar, why wouldn't you let us in? How glad I am to see you. Who would have thought of you?
BLUEBEARD. Why, Sybil, I hope you always thought of me.
SYBIL. Dear Uncle, so I do; but I meant to say of seeing you — I never dreamed I would while you were quartered here at . . . at . . . what is the name of this island anyway?

BLUEBEARD. (*lying*) I don't believe it has a name. I've never thought to give it one.

RODNEY. The sailors called it "The Island of Lost Love."

SYBIL. It's true our ship was almost lost in the fog.

RODNEY. And we are in love.

BLUEBEARD. (*aside*) Grrrr!

SYBIL. Oh, excuse me, Uncle, this is my fiancé, Rodney Parker.

BLUEBEARD. (*icily*) Howdyedo?

RODNEY. (*running off at the mouth*) Sybil has told me so much about you. She says you were the greatest misunderstood genius at medical school. But that you suddenly gave it all up, threw it all away to live here in almost total seclusion. . . .

SYBIL. (*interrupting*) And this is Miss Cubbidge, my beloved traveling companion and tutor.

MISS CUBBIDGE. (*shaking his hand violently*) I am incensed to meet you, Baron Bluebeard. Sybil told me that you were with her father at medical school when the terrible fire . . .

BLUEBEARD. (*flaring up*) Don't squeeze my hand! I work with my hands. (*then politely*) If you will excuse me. I expected only one guest. (*turning to MRS. MAGGOT and SHEEMISH, who bow with sinister smiles*) Now there are extra preparations to be made. Mrs. Maggot and Sheemish will show you to your rooms. (*kisses SYBIL's hand, shakes MISS CUBBIDGE's hand and ignores RODNEY's hand*) We will sup when the moon rises over Mount Agdora. (*exits*)

RODNEY. Did you see that? I offered him my hand, but he refused it.

SYBIL. I'm sure Uncle Khanazar meant nothing by it. He's so involved in his work and he's unused to human companionship.

Scene 8
SYBIL, RODNEY, CUBBIDGE, MAGGOT, SHEEMISH

RODNEY. (*aside to SYBIL*) What about these serving people he keeps around here?

SYBIL. (*aside to RODNEY and CUBBIDGE*) Yes, of course. (*then strangely*) But then they hardly seem human, do they?

MRS. MAGGOT. (*dykey*) This way to the washroom, ladies. Follow me to the washroom, ladies.

MISS CUBBIDGE. Shall we wash away that which we acquiesced during our long adjunct? I refer, of course, to the dust of travel.

SYBIL. Until dinner, Rodney dear.

RODNEY. Sybil, there is something that I must discuss with you.

SYBIL. Excuse me until then, dear Rodney, I must freshen up. (*throws him a kiss and exits*)

Scene 9
RODNEY, SHEEMISH

RODNEY. Ah, I'm convinced of it! Sybil is in love with him.

SHEEMISH. With whom?

RODNEY. Excuse me, I was thinking aloud. Thinking, thinking, thinking, that's all I ever do. My head thunders with thinking. I must stop thinking. I needs must shout it. (*very loud*) Why did she come here? To look for him. Nothing I could do but she must come to look for him. I think this jealousy will drive me mad!

SHEEMISH. Shall I tell you between our two selves

what I think of it? I'm afraid she'll get little return for her love; her journey to this foggy island will be useless.

RODNEY. (*overjoyed*) But what is the reason? Do tell me, Sheemish, what makes you take such a gloomy view of the situation?

SHEEMISH. His feelings are cold.

RODNEY. (*enraged again*) You think he will betray her innocent love?

SHEEMISH. He has no heart, that man.

RODNEY. But how could a gentleman do such a vile thing?

SHEEMISH. I have been his servant on this island 19 years and I will say this—just between us—that in my master, Baron Khanazar, the Bluebeard, you see the vilest scoundrel that ever cumbered the earth, a madman, a cur, a devil, a Turk, a heretic, who believes in neither Heaven, Hell, nor werewolf: he lives like an animal, like a swinish gourmet, a veritable vermin infesting his environs and shuttering his ears to every Christian remonstrance, and turning to ridicule everything we believe in.

RODNEY. But surely there's nothing between them. He wouldn't marry his own niece, Sybil. What a ridiculous idea! (*laughs*)

SHEEMISH. (*ominously and with candor*) Believe me, to satisfy his passion he would have gone further than that, he would have married you as well and her dog and cat into the bargain. Marriage means nothing to him. It is his usual method of ensnaring women! (*sound of footsteps*) But here he comes taking a turn in the palace. Let us separate—what I have spoken I have spoken in confidence. I am his slave, but a master who has given himself over to wickedness is a thing to be dreaded. If you repeat a word of this to him, I will swear you made it up. (*Exit RODNEY.*)

Scene 10
SHEEMISH, BLUEBEARD

BLUEBEARD. I have been in my laboratory putting things in readiness, for I have found the ideal subject for my next experiment . . . or should I say my next work of art?

SHEEMISH. (*with dread*) Oh, Master.

BLUEBEARD. What is it?

SHEEMISH. I'm afraid. I'm afraid. I'm afraid. (*leaps into BLUEBEARD's arms*)

BLUEBEARD. (*throwing him off*) Down, down, you fool. Never mind the disagreeable things that may happen. Let us think of the pleasant ones. This girl is almost the most charming creature imaginable. Add to that a few of my innovations! I never saw two people so devoted, so completely in love. The manifest tenderness of their mutual affection inspired a like feeling in me. It affected me deeply. My love began as jealousy. I couldn't bear to see them so happy together; vexation stimulated my desire and I realized what a pleasure it would give me to disturb their mutual understanding and break up an attachment so repugnant to my own susceptibilities.

SHEEMISH. Have you no desire for Miss Cubbidge?

BLUEBEARD. She is not without a certain cadaverous charm. (*footsteps*) Shhh! Quickly, the spy hole, see who it is.

SHEEMISH. The sun is in my eyes, but I know the sound of her footsteps. It is only Mrs. Maggot.

Scene 11
MRS. MAGGOT, SHEEMISH

MRS. MAGGOT and SHEEMISH bring on a table and chairs. Then they set the table for dinner.

MRS. MAGGOT. (*carrying in a platter*) Yum, yum, yum . . . I'm nibbling . . . yum . . . mutton good! Lovely . . . yum . . . yum . . . yum.

SHEEMISH. It is the first time meat has been seen in the palace for 19 years.

MRS. MAGGOT. Twenty for me! Twenty years and never any meat. I've withered. You fed yourself on the fat in your hump, didn't you? Ach. Ouf. (*She is seized by a violent coughing fit.*) Swallowed the wrong way.

SHEEMISH. Heaven has punished you, glutton. Stop, before you eat the knives and the tablecloth.

MRS. MAGGOT. My illness, not my sin! Look, Sheemish, a chicken! Ah, the drumstick! (*with her mouth full*) Those who have a stomach, eat; those who have a hump, glue themselves to keyholes.

SHEEMISH. Watch what you say to me. My hump contains a second brain to think my evil thoughts for me. It hasn't forgotten the broken test tube and our little secret.

MRS. MAGGOT. You must teach me to spy through keyholes. Which eye does one use, the right or the left? They say in time one's eye becomes shaped like a keyhole. I prefer eavesdropping. There, see my ear, a delicate shell. (*She shows her ear trumpet.*)

SHEEMISH. When others are present you are as deaf as a bat—but when we are alone you are cured and hear perfectly.

MRS. MAGGOT. It's a miracle! Look at that pork chop!

SHEEMISH. (*Grabs her and throws her onto the table. Climbing on top of her, he forces a huge piece of meat into her mouth.*) Here, glutton, eat this! Someday your mouth will be full of maggots and greenish pus. (*Laughter of the dinner guests is heard off.*) But here come the guests to dinner. Let us have a truce until the next time we are alone.

MRS. MAGGOT. Peace!

Scene 12
MRS. MAGGOT, SHEEMISH, BLUEBEARD, RODNEY, SYBIL, MISS CUBBIDGE

The dinner guests and BLUEBEARD enter. MRS. MAGGOT and SHEEMISH just manage to get off the table in the nick of time. MISS CUBBIDGE enters on BLUEBEARD's arm, SYBIL on RODNEY's arm.

BLUEBEARD. Work, work, work. I have thought of nothing else these 19 years. My work, my work, and nothing else.

SYBIL. Beware, Uncle, all work and no play makes Jack a dull boy.

MISS CUBBIDGE. True, Sybil, but all play and no work makes Jack a mere toy.

BLUEBEARD. No danger there. I never cease in my experimenting. My dream is to remake Man. A new man with new possibilities for love.

SYBIL. "Love for a man is a thing apart. 'Tis woman's whole existence."

MISS CUBBIDGE. (*applauding*) Lord Byron!

BLUEBEARD. Won't you all be seated? (*BLUEBEARD seats MISS CUBBIDGE at the table. RODNEY seats SYBIL.*)

MRS. MAGGOT. (*to SYBIL*) Why, dearie, what an unusual locket.

SYBIL. Yes. It's Lapis Lazuli. My Mother gave it to me the night she died when the terrible fire . . .

MISS CUBBIDGE. (*interrupting*) Don't, Sybil . . .

SYBIL. I never knew my mother.

RODNEY. Strange, all the places are set to one side of the table.

BLUEBEARD. That is because of a little surprise I have for you. There will be an entertainment tonight while we are taking our evening meal, a little play I wrote myself.

SYBIL. What, a play?

RODNEY. Jolly!

MISS CUBBIDGE. Wrote it yourself? You've a touch of erosion, I see, Baron. And yet you studied medicine?

BLUEBEARD. I write for amusement only.

MISS CUBBIDGE. Were you indoctrinated? I mean, did you receive the Doctorate? On what theme did you write your dissipation? Which degree did you receive?

BLUEBEARD. I received the third degree. (*MRS. MAGGOT places a platter of meat on the table.*)

RODNEY. This meat looks delicious.

BLUEBEARD. (*having a seizure*) Meat? Meat? (*turning on MRS. MAGGOT*) You dare to serve them meat?

MRS. MAGGOT. Eh?

BLUEBEARD. (*in a blind rage*) Take it away at once, blockhead! Do you want to ruin my experiment? (*He throws the meat at MRS. MAGGOT and then leaps up on the dinner table like a wild man, roaring.*) What is the Law?

MRS. MAGGOT and SHEEMISH. (*Bowing before him as though he were an idol on an altar, they link their arms together and chant, swaying back and forth rhythmically.*) We are not men. We are not women. We are not men. We are not women. He is the hand that makes. We are not men. We are not women. His is the House of Pain. We are not men. We are not women. This is the Law!

BLUEBEARD. (*rolling his eyes savagely*) Now get out! (*turning on the guests*) All of you!

MISS CUBBIDGE. (*horrified*) What about dinner?

BLUEBEARD. I've lost my appetite!

RODNEY. What about the play?
BLUEBEARD. I detest avant-garde theater.

SCENE 13
*BLUEBEARD, MISS CUBBIDGE, SYBIL,
RODNEY, SHEEMISH, MRS. MAGGOT, LAMIA*

The face of LAMIA THE LEOPARD WOMAN, appears at the window.

RODNEY. Look, there's a face at the window!

(*MISS CUBBIDGE screams. SYBIL faints in RODNEY's arms. BLUEBEARD fires his revolver at LAMIA: Tableau vivant. The curtain falls.*)

ACT II

SCENE 1
SYBIL, RODNEY

SYBIL. Rodney, you have come to speak to me about my letter to you.

RODNEY. Yes, you could have told me face to face. People living in the same house, even when they are the only people living on a deserted island, as we are, can be further apart than if they lived 50 miles asunder in the country.

SYBIL. I have thought much of what I then wrote and I feel sure that we had better . . .

RODNEY. Stop, Sybil . . . do not speak hurriedly, love. Shall I tell you what I learned from your letter?

SYBIL. Yes, tell me if you think it is better that you should do so.

RODNEY. I learned that something had made you melancholy since we came to this island. There are few of us who do not encounter, every now and again, some of that irrational spirit of sadness which, when overindulged, leads men to madness and self-destruction. Since I have loved you I have banished it utterly. Do not speak under the influence of that spirit until you have thought whether you too can banish it.

SYBIL. I have tried, but it will not be banished.

RODNEY. Try again, Sybil, if you love me. If you do not . . .

SYBIL. If I do not love you, I love no one upon earth. (*sits quietly, looking into his face*)

RODNEY. I believe it. I believe it as I believe in my own love for you. I trust your love implicitly, Sybil. So come, return with me to the mainland and let us make an early marriage.

SYBIL. (*strangely, as if in a trance*) No, I cannot do so.

RODNEY. (*smiling*) Is that melancholy fiend too much for you? Sybil, Sybil, Sybil.

SYBIL. (*snapping out of it*) You are noble, good, and great. I find myself unfit to be your wife.

RODNEY. Don't quibble, Sybil.

SYBIL. (*falling to her knees*) I beg your pardon on my knees.

RODNEY. I grant no such pardon. Do you think I will let you go from me in that way? No, love, if you are ill, I will wait till your illness is gone by; and if you will let me, I will be your nurse.

SYBIL. I am not ill. (*Her hands stray unconsciously to her breasts and yoni.*)

RODNEY. Not ill with any defined sickness. You do not shake with ague, nor does your head rack you with aching; but yet you must be ill to try to put an end to all that has passed between us for no reason at all.

SYBIL. (*standing suddenly*) Mr. Parker . . .

RODNEY. (*deeply hurt*) If you will call me so, I will think it only part of your malady.

SYBIL. Mr. Parker, I can only hope that you will take me at my word. I beg your forgiveness and that our engagement may be over.

RODNEY. No, no, no, Sybil. Never with my consent. I would marry you tomorrow, tomorrow or next month, or the month after. But if it cannot be so, then I will wait . . . unless . . . there is some other man. Yes, that! and that alone would convince me. Only your marriage to another man could convince me that I had lost you. (*He kisses her on the lips.*)

SYBIL. (*turning away and surreptitiously wiping away the kiss*) I cannot convince you in that way.

RODNEY. (*Prissily wipes his lips on a lace hanky, and carefully folds it and replaces it in his breast pocket, relieved.*) You will convince me in no other. Have you spoken to your uncle of this yet?

SYBIL. Not as yet.

RODNEY. (*anxiously*) Do not tell him. It is possible you may have to unsay what you have said.

SYBIL. No, it is not possible.

RODNEY. I think you must leave this island. The foggy air is no good for you. You need the sun, I think. You've grown so pale. You need a change.

SYBIL. Yes, you treat me as though I were partly silly and partly insane, but it is not so. The change you speak of should be in my nature and in yours. (*Rodney shakes his head and smiles. Aside.*) He is perfect! Oh, that he were less perfect!

RODNEY. I'll leave you alone for 24 hours to think this over. I advise you not to tell your uncle. But if you do tell him, let me know that you have done so.

SYBIL. Why that?

RODNEY. (*pressing her hand*) Good night, dearest, dearest Sybil. (*exits*)

SCENE 2
SYBIL, BLUEBEARD

BLUEBEARD. What, Sybil, are you not in bed yet?

SYBIL. Not yet, Uncle Khanazar.

BLUEBEARD. So Rodney Parker has been here. I smell his cologne in the air.

SYBIL. Yes, he has been here.

BLUEBEARD. Is anything the matter, Sybil?

SYBIL. No, Uncle Khanazar, nothing is the matter.

BLUEBEARD. He has not made himself disagreeable, has he?

SYBIL. Not in the least. He never does anything wrong. He may defy man or woman to find fault with him.

BLUEBEARD. So that's it, is it? He is just a shade too good. I have noticed that myself. But it's a fault on the right side.

SYBIL. (*deeply troubled*) It's no fault, Uncle. If there be any fault, it is not with him.

BLUEBEARD. Being too good is not one of my faults. . . . I am very bad.

SYBIL. (*starry-eyed*) Are you bad? Are you really bad?

BLUEBEARD. When I am good, I am very, very good; but when I'm bad, I'm not bad. I'm good at being bad. . . . I do it well.

SYBIL. (*again as if in a trance*) Tonight, at dinner, your words carried me away . . . (*Their lips almost meet but she yawns, breaking the spell, and he yawns sympathetically.*) . . . But I am yawning and tired and I will go to bed. Good night, Uncle Khanazar.

BLUEBEARD. Good night, Sybil. (*Aside*) And rest, for a new life awaits you! (*Exit SYBIL.*)

SCENE 3
BLUEBEARD, MISS CUBBIDGE

MISS CUBBIDGE. Oh, excuse me. I didn't realize that the parlor was preoccupied. (*starts out*)

BLUEBEARD. Come in, Miss Cubbidge. I do not desire to be alone.

Miss Cubbidge. No, I think I'd better go and leave you to your own devices.

Bluebeard. Please stay. I think I know what you are thinking.

Miss Cubbidge. I'll do my own thinking, thank you; and my own existing.

Bluebeard. Miss Cubbidge, I don't think you like me.

Miss Cubbidge. I can sympathize with neither your virtues nor your vices.

Bluebeard. What would you say if I told you that I need a wife?

Miss Cubbidge. I do not believe in sudden marriages.

Bluebeard. People often say that marriage is an important thing and should be much thought of in advance, and marrying people are cautioned that there are many who marry in haste and repent at leisure. I am not sure, however, that marriage may not be pondered over too much; nor do I feel certain that the leisurely repentance does not as often follow the leisurely marriages as it does the rapid ones. Why, you yourself might marry suddenly (*kneeling before her on one knee*) and never regret it at all.

Miss Cubbidge. My health might fail me under the effects of so great a change made so late in life.

Bluebeard. Miss Cubbidge, how can you live without love?

Miss Cubbidge. It is my nature to love many persons a little if I've loved few or none passionately, Baron Bluebeard.

Bluebeard. Please, call me Khanazar; and may I call you . . .

Miss Cubbidge. (*shyly*) Flora.

Bluebeard. Ah, Flora! It is only possible to be alone with you in nature. All other women destroy the landscape; you alone become part of it.

Miss Cubbidge. (*aside*) Could any woman resist such desuetude? (*giggling*) Why, Baron Blue . . .

Bluebeard. (*interrupting*) Khanazar.

Miss Cubbidge. (*giggling*) Khanazar.

Bluebeard. Flora, you are part of the trees, the sky; you are the dominating goddess of nature. Come to me, Flora, you lovely little fauna, you.

Miss Cubbidge. (*recovering herself*) Mr. Bluebeard, I shall certainly not come to you.

Bluebeard. (*suddenly*) Look, do you see what it is I am holding in my hand?

Miss Cubbidge. (*alarmed*) A revolver!

Bluebeard. Take it, press it to my temple and shoot, or say you will be mine.

Miss Cubbidge. (*Frightened with the revolver in her hand.*) I can't shoot you, but I cannot be yours, either.

Bluebeard. It is one or the other. Blow my brains out. I will not live another day without you.

Miss Cubbidge. Recuperate your gun at once. It isn't loaded, is it?

Bluebeard. Pull the trigger! There are worse things awaiting Man than death.

Miss Cubbidge. To what do you collude?

Bluebeard. All tortures do not matter . . . only not to be dead before one dies. I will not live without your love. (*He pretends to weep.*)

Miss Cubbidge. Don't weep, Baron Bluebeard . . . er . . . Khanazar. 'Tisn't manly. Try to be more malevolent.

Bluebeard. Marry me, marry me, Flora, and make me the happiest man on earth.

Miss Cubbidge. How can I marry you?

Bluebeard. (*hypnotically*) Easily. Just repeat after me. I, Flora Cubbidge . . .

MISS CUBBIDGE. I, Flora Cubbidge . . .

BLUEBEARD. Do solemnly swear . . .

MISS CUBBIDGE. Do solemnly swear . . .

BLUEBEARD. To take this man, Baron Khanazar von Bluebeard, as my lawful wedded husband . . .

MISS CUBBIDGE. To take this man, Baron Khanazar von Bluebeard, as my lawful wedded husband . . .

BLUEBEARD. To love, honor, and obey; for better or for worse; for richer or poorer; in sickness and in health; from this day forward . . . (*He begins to undress her.*)

MISS CUBBIDGE. To love, honor, and obey; for better or for worse; for richer or for poorer; in sickness and in health; from this day forward . . .

BLUEBEARD. Until death us do part.

MISS CUBBIDGE. Till death us do part.

BLUEBEARD. (*licentiously*) I may now kiss the bride.

MISS CUBBIDGE. What about your vows?

BLUEBEARD. Don't you trust me?

MISS CUBBIDGE. I do. I do. I do. (*They begin to breathe heavily as they undress slowly. They move toward each other, wearing only their shoes, socks, stockings and her merry widow. They clinch and roll about on the floor making animal noises.*)

BLUEBEARD. Was ever woman in this manner wooed? Was ever woman in this manner won?

MISS CUBBIDGE. (*aside*) There are things that happen in a day that would take a lifetime to explain.

(*There follows a scene of unprecedented eroticism in which MISS CUBBIDGE gives herself voluptuously to BARON VON BLUEBEARD.*)

BLUEBEARD. In my right pants pocket you will find a

key. It is the key to my laboratory. Take it. And swear to me that you will never use it.

MISS CUBBIDGE. I swear! I must return to Sybil at once. She sometimes wakes up in a phalanx.

BLUEBEARD. Won't you sleep here tonight, with me?

MISS CUBBIDGE. No, I can't sleep in this bed. It has cold, wet spots in it. Good night, Baron . . . husband.

BLUEBEARD. Good night, Miss Cubbidge.

MISS CUBBIDGE. Please don't mention our hymeneals to Sybil. I must find the right words to immure the news to her.

BLUEBEARD. Believe me, I'll confess to none of it.

MISS CUBBIDGE. Thank you. I believe that you have transformed me to a part of the dirigible essence. You have carried me aloft and I believe I am with Beatrice, of whom Dante has sung in his immortal onus. Good night. (*exit*)

SCENE 4
BLUEBEARD

BLUEBEARD. It is a lucky thing for me that I did not take the vows or this marriage might be binding on me as it is on her. I cannot sleep tonight. There is work to be done in my laboratory. Good night, Miss Cubbidge, wherever you are. And good night to all the ladies who do be living in this world. Good night, ladies. Good night, sweet ladies. (*exits into laboratory*)

SCENE 5
RODNEY PARKER, LAMIA THE LEOPARD WOMAN, MRS. MAGGOT

Entering surreptitiously, MRS. MAGGOT crosses lighting the candelabra.

LAMIA. SHHH! Take care or the deaf one. . . . She hears nothing of what you shout and overhears everything that you whisper.

RODNEY. What is it that you wish to tell me?

LAMIA. He is mad, I tell you, mad! And he will stop at nothing.

RODNEY. Who?

LAMIA. The Bluebeard, Khanazar. If you love that girl, convince her to leave this island at once.

RODNEY. But why?

LAMIA. Look at me. I was a woman once!

RODNEY. But you are a woman. So very much a woman. You are all woman.

LAMIA. No, no, never again will I bear the name of woman. I was changed in the House of Pain. I was a victim of his sex-switch tricks and his queer quackery.

RODNEY. Quackery—Sybil told me that he was a brilliant physiologist.

LAMIA. Even in Denmark they called him a quack. He wasn't satisfied with sex switches. He wants to create a third genital organ attached between the legs of a third sex. I am an experiment that failed.

RODNEY. (*seductively*) You look like a woman to me.

LAMIA. I wish I could be a woman to you. (*aside*) Perhaps when Bluebeard is defeated I will. (*aloud*) He uses the same technique on all his victims. First he married me. Then he gave me the key to his laboratory, forbidding me to ever use it. Then he waited for curiosity to get the better of me. All women are curious.

RODNEY. Men marry because they are tired, women because they are curious.

LAMIA. Both are disappointed.

RODNEY. Does he ever use men for his experiments?

LAMIA. At first he did. Sheemish was the first. But when that experiment failed he turned to women. We are all experiments that have failed. He has made us the slaves of this island.

RODNEY. (*realizing*) The Island of Lost Love.

LAMIA. Save yourself and save the woman you love. Take the advice of the Leopard Woman and go.

RODNEY. How did a nice girl like you get mixed up in a mess like this?

LAMIA. I was entertaining in a small bistro nightclub called The Wild Cat's Pussy. I was billed as Lamia the Leopard Woman. It was only 14 beans a day but I needed the scratch. I sang this song: (*sings*)
Where is my Leopard Lover?
When will I spot the cat for me?
I'm wild when I'm under cover.
Where is the cat who will tame me?
Where is my wild cat lover?
Leopard hunting is all the rage.
Where is my wild cat lover?
I'm free but I want to be caged.
If you dig this feline,
Better make a bee-line.
I've got the spots to give men the red-
 hots
Where is my wild leopard hunter?
I'm game if you'll play my game.
Where is that runt cunt hunter?
I'm wild but I want to be tame.
After I sang my set, he signaled and I sat at his table. He ordered a Tiger's Milk Flip. He was into health food. No woman can resist him, I tell you.

RODNEY. He seduced you?

LAMIA. Worst, worst, a thousand times worst. I didn't know if I was coming or going. He has a way with women.

RODNEY. Sybil, great Scott no. Either you're jesting or I'm dreaming! Sybil with another man? I'll go mad.

LAMIA. His idealism . . . his intensity . . . the Clairol blue of his beard! His words carried me away. He had a strange look in his eyes. I felt strange inside. He and I were total strangers! If you love her, get her off this island before it is too late.

RODNEY. No, not Sybil. I am ashamed to listen to you. Yet she admires him so. . . . I have gone mad!

LAMIA. He came closer . . . closer. "Submit," he said, "in the name of science and the dark arts. Submit. Submit."

RODNEY. (*in a panic*) Sybil is with him now. You are lying.

LAMIA. If you think I am lying, look. (*She lifts her sarong.*) Look what he did to the Leopard Woman's pussy.

RODNEY. Eeeccht! Is that a mound of Venus or a penis?

LAMIA. (*perplexed*) I wish I knew.

RODNEY. No, no, he can't do that to Sybil. I must kill him. What am I saying? This is madness. But what conclusion is sanity to me? The most faithful of women is after all only a woman. I'll kill you. No, I am mad.

LAMIA. Go and stop him. Save her from the fate that has befallen me.

RODNEY. I will kill myself! No, I will kill her! Oh, God, it is impossible. I have gone mad! (*He runs out.*)

SCENE 6
LAMIA

LAMIA. (*sings*)
I've lost my leopard lover.

A world of made is not a world of
   born.
Bluebeard will soon discover
Hell hath no fury like a woman
   scorned.

Scene 7
LAMIA, SHEEMISH

LAMIA. (*calling after him*) Rodney! Rodney! Rodney! He is gone.

SHEEMISH. (*appearing out of the shadows*) Are you afraid of being alone?

LAMIA. (*fanning herself with a leopard fan*) How stifling it is! There must be a storm coming.

SHEEMISH. I heard you telling the secrets of the island to Rodney (*spits*) Parker.

LAMIA. (*furiously*) Sneaking little eavesdropper! How dare you?

SHEEMISH. I love you.

LAMIA. (*fanning herself*) What awful weather! This is the second day of it.

SHEEMISH. Every day I walk four miles to see you and four miles back and meet with nothing but indifference from you.

LAMIA. Your love touches me but I can't return it, that's all.

SHEEMISH. (*accusing*) But you came four miles here to tell the secrets of the island to Rodney (*Spits*) Parker.

LAMIA. You are a bore.

SHEEMISH. (*twisting her arm*) You are in love with him!

LAMIA. (*in pain*) Yes, its true. If you must know. I do

love him. I do! (*aside*) For all the good it will do me. He loves Sybil.

SHEEMISH. (*taking her in his arms roughly and humping her like a dog*) I want you.

LAMIA. (*fighting him*) You stupid, vulgar, deformed nincompoop! Do you think I could ever fall for such a one as you? You are as ugly as sin itself. Besides, our genitals would never fit together.

SHEEMISH. (*groping her*) We can work it out.

LAMIA. Evil cretin! God will punish you. (*She breaks away.*)

SHEEMISH. God will not punish the lunatic soul. He knows the powers of evil are too great for us with weak minds. Marry me!

LAMIA. I'd rather blow a bald baboon with B.O. and bunions than marry a monster! (*Exit LAMIA in a huff.*)

SHEEMISH. (*following her*) Lamia, be reasonable!

SCENE 8
BLUEBEARD, SYBIL

SYBIL is seated at the spinet. She plays dramatic music. BLUEBEARD moves slowly, approaching her from behind. His eyes are ablaze. She senses, his approach. She plays with greater emphasis. Her shoulders are bare. He begins kissing them. The music she is playing rises to a crescendo. She stops playing suddenly.

SYBIL. This is ridiculous!

BLUEBEARD. (*swinging a key on a chain back and forth before her eyes as though hypnotizing her*) Here is the key to my laboratory. Take it and swear to me that you will never use it.

SYBIL. (*in a trance*) Yes, Master!

BLUEBEARD. Ah, my darling, my own one. You will be my wife.

SYBIL. Yes, Master!

BLUEBEARD. You will be the loveliest of all wives. (*aside*) When I am through with you.

SYBIL. Yes, Master.

BLUEBEARD. I am about to perform the *magnum opus.* The creation of a third genital organ will perhaps lead to the creation of a third sex. You will be my ultimate masterpiece of vivisection! (*He kisses her.*)

SCENE 9
BLUEBEARD, SYBIL, CUBBIDGE

MISS CUBBIDGE. (*entering*) Sir, what are you doing with Sybil there? Are you making love to her too?

BLUEBEARD. (*aside to CUBBIDGE*) No, no, on the contrary, she throws herself at me shamelessly, although I tell her that I am married to you.

SYBIL. What is it you want, Miss Cubbidge?

BLUEBEARD. (*aside to SYBIL*) She is jealous of my speaking to you. She wants me to marry her, but I tell her it is you I must have.

MISS CUBBIDGE. (*incredulous*) What, Sybil?

BLUEBEARD. (*Aside to CUBBIDGE*) The impressionable little creature is infatuated with me.

SYBIL. (*incredulous*) What, Miss Cubbidge?

BLUEBEARD. (*aside to SYBIL*) The desperate old maid has got her claws out for me.

MISS CUBBIDGE. Do you . . .

BLUEBEARD 33

BLUEBEARD. (*to MISS CUBBIDGE*) Your words would be in vain.

SYBIL. I'd . . .

BLUEBEARD. (*to SYBIL*) All you can say to her will be in vain.

MISS CUBBIDGE. Truly . . .

BLUEBEARD. (*aside to CUBBIDGE*) She's obstinate as the devil.

SYBIL. I think . . .

BLUEBEARD. (*aside to SYBIL*) Say nothing to her. She's a madwoman.

SYBIL. No, no, I must speak to her.

MISS CUBBIDGE. I'll hear her reasons.

SYBIL. What . . .

BLUEBEARD. (*aside to SYBIL*) I'll lay you a wager she tells you she's my wife.

MISS CUBBIDGE. I . . .

BLUEBEARD. (*aside to CUBBIDGE*) I'll bet you she says I'm going to marry her.

MISS CUBBIDGE. Sybil, as your chaperone I must intercept. It is past your bedtime.

SYBIL. Dear Miss Cubbidge, I have been to bed but I got up because I have insomnia.

MISS CUBBIDGE. So I see. Sybil, I must ask you to leave me alone with *my* husband. The Baron and I married ourselves in an improvident ceremony earlier this evening.

BLUEBEARD. (*aside to SYBIL*) What did I tell you? She's out of her mind.

SYBIL. Dear *Miss* Cubbidge, are you sure you are feeling all right? Are you ill?

MISS CUBBIDGE. (*indignantly*) I've never felt more supine in my life. Sybil, it does not become a young *unmarried* woman to meddle in the affairs of others.

BLUEBEARD. (*aside to CUBBIDGE*) She thinks she is going to marry me.

SYBIL. It is not fit, *Miss* Cubbidge, to be jealous because the Baron speaks to me. I am going to be his wife.

BLUEBEARD. (*aside to CUBBIDGE*) What did I tell you?

SYBIL. Baron, did you not promise to marry me?

BLUEBEARD. (*aside to SYBIL*) Of course, my darling.

MISS CUBBIDGE. Baron, am I not your wife, the Baroness von Bluebeard?

BLUEBEARD. (*aside to CUBBIDGE*) How could you ask such a question?

SYBIL. (*aside to the audience*) How sure the old goat is of herself!

MISS CUBBIDGE. (*aside to the audience*) The Baron is right, how pig-headed the little bitch is!

SYBIL. We must know the truth.

MISS CUBBIDGE. We must have the matter abnegated.

SYBIL *and* MISS CUBBIDGE. Which of us will it be, Baron?

BLUEBEARD. (*addressing himself to both of them*) What would you have me say? Each of you knows in your heart of hearts whether or not I have made love to you. Let her that I truly love laugh at what the other says. Actions speak louder than words. (*aside to CUBBIDGE*) Let her believe what she will. (*aside to SYBIL*) Let her flatter herself in your senile imagination. (*aside to CUBBIDGE*) I adore you. (*aside to SYBIL*) I am yours alone. (*aside to CUBBIDGE*) One night with you is worth a thousand with other women. (*aside to SYBIL*) All faces are ugly in your presence. (*aloud*) If you will excuse me, there's work to be done in my laboratory. I do not wish to be disturbed. Good night, ladies. (*exits*)

Scene 10
SYBIL, MISS CUBBIDGE, SHEEMISH

SHEEMISH. (*appearing out of the shadows*) Poor ladies! I can't bear to see you led to your destruction. Take my advice, return to the mainland.
SYBIL. I am she he loves, however.
MISS CUBBIDGE. It is to me he's married.
SHEEMISH. My master is an evil sadist. He will do you irreparable harm as he has done to others. He wants to marry the whole female sex so that he can take them to his laboratory and . . .

Scene 11
*SYBIL, MISS CUBBIDGE,
SHEEMISH, BLUEBEARD*

BLUEBEARD. (*popping back in*) One more word . . .
SHEEMISH. My master is no evil sadist. He means you no harm. If you ladies think he can marry the whole female sex, you've got another think coming. He is a man of his word. There he is—ask him yourself.
BLUEBEARD. What were you saying, Sheemish?
SHEEMISH. (*aside to BLUEBEARD*) You know how catty women are. I was defending you . . . as best I could.
BLUEBEARD. (*to SYBIL and MISS CUBBIDGE*) She who holds the key to my heart holds the key to my laboratory. (*exit*)

Scene 12
MISS CUBBIDGE, SYBIL, SHEEMISH

MISS CUBBIDGE. (*aside*) Then he is my husband, for he gave me the key.

36 BLUEBEARD

SYBIL. (*aside*) The key, I have the key! It is me he loves after all. (*loud*) Good night, Madame. If you have the key, you are his wife.

MISS CUBBIDGE. Good night, Sybil. If it is to you he gave the key, you are his bethrothed. (*They both exit laughing*)

SCENE 13
SHEEMISH, MRS. MAGGOT

MRS. MAGGOT. (*entering excitedly*) I overheard laughter. It is the first time laughter has been heard on this island in 19 years. Who was laughing? Who is it that knows a single moment of happiness on the Island of Lost Love?

SHEEMISH. It was not with joy you heard them laughing, but with scorn. Bluebeard has got the young woman and her governess fighting like cats in the alley.

MRS. MAGGOT. I thought they always swore by each other.

SHEEMISH. It's at each other that they swear now. He's married both of them!

SCENE 14
SHEEMISH, MRS. MAGGOT, SYBIL

MRS. MAGGOT. Look, here comes the young one carrying a candle, her long black hair unloosed, her lips slightly parted. A lovely flower that blooms for just one hour.

SHEEMISH. A sleepwalker, a somnambulist.

MRS. MAGGOT. Her eyes are open.

SHEEMISH. But their sense is shut. I believe he has mesmerized her. Let us conceal ourselves, I will keep my eyes peeled.

MRS. MAGGOT. And I my ears. I can't wait to find out what happens next! (*MRS. MAGGOT and SHEEMISH hide.*)

SYBIL. I can control my curiosity no longer. I must see what lies behind the door to my lover's laboratory. I know he has forbade me ever to use this key. But how can I stand the suspense? Should not a woman take an interest in her husband's work? (*She unlocks the door with her key and opens it. BLUEBEARD awaits her.*)

MRS. MAGGOT. Shouldn't we try to save her?

SHEEMISH. Would you prefer to take her place in the House of Pain?

MRS. MAGGOT. No, no, not the House of Pain.

SCENE 15
SYBIL, BLUEBEARD, SHEEMISH, MRS. MAGGOT

BLUEBEARD. I trust you have kept your coming here a secret.

SYBIL. Baron!

BLUEBEARD. Curiosity killed the cat. (*aside*) But it may have a salutary effect on the pussy. Look into my eyes, my little kitten, and repeat after me. (*hypnotizing her*) I, Sybil, do solemnly swear to take this man, Baron Khanazar von Bluebeard, as my lawful wedded husband.

SYBIL. I, Sybil, do solemnly swear to take this man, Baron Khanazar von Bluebeard, as my lawful wedded husband.

MRS. MAGGOT. (*moving her ear trumpet like an an-*

tenna) I hear someone coming. Just in time! Rodney Parker will save her from the fate worse than death!

SHEEMISH. (*aside*) My rival, Rodney Parker! Now I will have my revenge. (*to MRS. MAGGOT*) Detain him!

BLUEBEARD. To love, honor and obey . . .

MRS. MAGGOT. Oh, cruel! Don't ask me that. I won't do it. Anything but that.

SYBIL. To love, honor and obey.

SHEEMISH. Even the House of Pain? The test tube! Master, Master . . .

BLUEBEARD. For better or for worse; for richer or for poorer . . .

MRS. MAGGOT. I'll do it.

BLUEBEARD. In sickness and in health . . . from this day forward . . .

SYBIL. For better or for worse; for richer or for poorer . . . in sickness and in health, from this day forward . . .

SCENE 16
SHEEMISH, MRS. MAGGOT, SYBIL, BLUEBEARD, RODNEY

RODNEY rushes onto the stage, mad.

RODNEY. Where is he? Where is he?

(*SHEEMISH roughly throws MRS. MAGGOT into RODNEY.*)

MRS. MAGGOT. Eh?
BLUEBEARD. Until death us do part.
SYBIL. Until death us do part.

BLUEBEARD 39

(*BLUEBEARD blows out the candle and kisses SYBIL.*)

RODNEY. (*shaking MRS. MAGGOT violently*) Where is Bluebeard?
MRS. MAGGOT. Eh?
RODNEY. Aagh! (*He throws MRS. MAGGOT aside.*)
BLUEBEARD. (*pressing SYBIL to him, demented*) And now, ye demons, ere this night goes by,
I swear I'll conjure or I'll die!
RODNEY. (*sees BLUEBEARD*) Damn you, Bluebeard! Damn your soul!
SYBIL. Rodney! Ah! (*She faints.*)

(*BLUEBEARD catches her and quickly carries her into the laboratory. MRS. MAGGOT trips RODNEY, then SHEEMISH and MRS. MAGGOT follow, slamming the door in RODNEY's face and locking it. RODNEY beats on the door and shouts.*)

SCENE 17
RODNEY

RODNEY. Open the door, you pervert! You invert, you necrophiliac! Open up! Bluebeard! Bluebeard! BLUEBEARD!

Curtain

ACT III

SCENE 1
BLUEBEARD, SYBIL, SHEEMISH, MRS. MAGGOT

There is no lapse of time between Act II and Act III. The scene changes to the interior of BLUEBEARD's laboratory. Enter BLUEBEARD carrying SYBIL in his arms. He walks with a hesitant step, looking from side to side, his cheeks quivering, contracting and expanding, his eyes intently focused. SHEEMISH and MRS. MAGGOT scurry about taking care of last-minute details. There is an air of great anticipation.

RODNEY'S VOICE. (*offstage*) Bluebeard! Bluebeard! Bluebeard! Open this door or I'll break it down! (*loud knocking*) Bluebeard!

BLUEBEARD. (*laughing*) That door is lined with double-duty quilted zinc. No mortal arm can break it down. Even a man whose heart is pure and has the strength of ten could not break it down. But a delicate girl with just enough strength to lift a powder-puff to her white bosom can open it . . . if she has the key. (*more loud knocking*) Sheemish, take the girl to the operating room, bathe her and prepare her for surgery.

SHEEMISH. No, Master, please don't ask me to do that. Anything but that.

BLUEBEARD. And be gentle with her. I want no marks left on her lily-white body. If you so much as bruise her, you and I will make an appointment for a meeting here in the House of Pain, hum?

BLUEBEARD 41

SHEEMISH. No, no, not the House of Pain! (*He carries SYBIL off.*)

SCENE 2
BLUEBEARD, MRS. MAGGOT

BLUEBEARD. Mrs. Maggot, bring in the frog, the serpent and the hearts, hands, eyes, feet, but most of all the blood and genitals of the little children. Bring in the serpent first. I need it to trace a magic circle.

MRS. MAGGOT. Eh?

BLUEBEARD. Perhaps your hearing would be improved by a vacation. (*He covers her ears and whispers.*) In the House of Pain.

MRS. MAGGOT. No, no, not the House of Pain!

(*She quickly hands him a bottle of blood and a paintbrush.*)

BLUEBEARD. (*laughs*) Thank you. Now leave me. Go and assist Sheemish. (*MRS. MAGGOT lingers.*) Is there something that you want, Maggot?

MRS. MAGGOT. Yes, Master.

BLUEBEARD. Well, what is it?

MRS. MAGGOT. The lapis lazuli locket the girl is wearing. May I have it?

BLUEBEARD. Yes, take it, scavenger!

MRS. MAGGOT. Do you think she will mind?

BLUEBEARD. No, she will not mind. She will remember nothing of her former life after the operation. Now get out. (*kicks her in the ass*)

MRS. MAGGOT. Thank you, thank you, Master. (*exit*)

Scene 3
BLUEBEARD

BLUEBEARD. (*enscribing a circle of blood*)
Now by the powers that only seem to be,
With crystal sword and flame I conjure thee.
I kiss the book; oh come to me!
Goddess of night: Hecate!

(*The sound of a gong is heard and a high-pitched cock crow that sometimes breaks from the most refined throat. HECATE appears in a flash of light and a puff of smoke.*)

Scene 4
BLUEBEARD, HECATE

HECATE. (*wearing a blue beard*) Who summons the Slave of Sin?

BLUEBEARD. (*laughing quietly aside*) Not for nothing I have worshipped the Dark One. (*to HECATE*) I called, Hecate; I, Khanazar von Bluebeard.

HECATE. How dare you? Don't you know that torture is the price you pay for summoning the Slave of Sin?

BLUEBEARD. All tortures do not matter: only not to be dead before one dies.

HECATE. What is it you want of me, my fool?

BLUEBEARD. Look, here are my books written in blood, there my apparatus. For 19 long years I've waited and worked for this moment. In there, on the operating table, swathed in bandages, a new sex, waiting to live again in a genital I made with my own hands! (*manically*) With my own hands!

HECATE. What about your own genitalia?

BLUEBEARD. The male genital organ is but a faint relic and shadow, a sign that has become detached from its substance and lives on as an exquisite ornament.

HECATE. And what do you want of me, my fool?

BLUEBEARD. Good fortune.

HECATE. Do not seek your good fortune. You carry on your forehead the sign of the elect.

Seek, probe,

Details unfold.

Let nature's secret

Be retold.

If ever you mean to try, you should try now. (*She vanishes.*)

(*There is a roll of thunder. Dramatic music from Bartok's* Castle of Bluebeard *begins to swell. BLUEBEARD dons surgeon's coat, gloves and mask and enters the House of Pain. MRS. MAGGOT and SHEEMISH close the doors after him. There is the sound of loud knocking at the door.*)

Scene 5
MRS. MAGGOT, SHEEMISH

MRS. MAGGOT. Look, Sheemish, the lapis lazuli locket. The Master said I could have it. Pretty, ain't it?

SHEEMISH. What's with you and that locket? (*A bloodcurdling scream issues from the laboratory. We may be sure that it is SYBIL writhing under the vivisector's knife. Both SHEEMISH and MRS. MAGGOT freeze for a moment in terror and clutch their own genitals in sympathy.*) Listen, he has begun the operation.

(*There is another bloodcurdling scream. Again MRS. MAGGOT and SHEEMISH freeze and clutch their genitals.*)

RODNEY'S VOICE. (*off*) What are you doing in there, you monster? (*He beats loudly on the door. SYBIL screams again off.*) Open the door or I'll tear your heart out! (*knocks loudly*)

SCENE 6
BLUEBEARD, MAGGOT, SHEEMISH

BLUEBEARD. (*rushes on*) The test tube! The test tube. Everything depends upon the sticky liquid now. (*He snatches the test tube and hurries back to his work.*)

(*MRS. MAGGOT and SHEEMISH exchange a guilty look. Another scream is heard. Suddenly MISS CUBBIDGE and RODNEY burst into the room. MISS CUBBIDGE brandishes the key.*)

SCENE 7
MRS. MAGGOT, SHEEMISH, RODNEY, MISS CUBBIDGE

MISS CUBBIDGE. I could control my curiosity no longer.
RODNEY. I'll see to it that he goes to the guillotine. That will shorten him by a head.
MISS CUBBIDGE. He robbed me of my maiden-head. So it's not his head I'll see cut off him! I want him decalced. (*Another scream is heard.*)

RODNEY. Let me at him. I'll maim the bloody bugger.

SHEEMISH. Don't be a fool. The girl is on the operating table. If you interfere now, she'll lose her life.

MISS CUBBIDGE. (*Aside*) With Sybil out of the way, the Baron will be mine alone. (*Aloud*) We must save her no matter what the danger. (*SYBIL screams again.*)

RODNEY. I can't stand it. I'm going in there.

SHEEMISH. Are you crazy?

RODNEY. Yes, I'm crazy.

SHEEMISH. Can't you understand that we are powerless against a supernatural enemy?

SCENE 8
BLUEBEARD, MISS CUBBIDGE, RODNEY, MRS. MAGGOT, SHEEMISH

BLUEBEARD. The time has come. The final stage of transmutation must be completed. Mars, God of War, and Venus, Goddess of Love, are conjunct in the twelfth house. The house of change and transformation. Scorpio, which rules surgery and the genitalia, is at the zenith. This is the horoscope I have been waiting for. The signs are in perfect aspect. The third genital will be born under the most beneficent stars that twinkle in the heavens. Sheemish, bring in the girl, or should I say "subject"?

MISS CUBBIDGE. Khanazar, you have deceived me. I . . .

BLUEBEARD. Quiet! I have no time to talk to an idiot.

RODNEY. If anything goes wrong with this experiment, I swear I'll kill you.

BLUEBEARD. I have already sworn upon the cross to enter into this experiment for life and for death.

(*SHEEMISH carries on SYBIL, who is wrapped in bandages like a mummy.*)

Scene 9
RODNEY, SYBIL, SHEEMISH, MISS CUBBIDGE, MRS. MAGGOT, BLUEBEARD

BLUEBEARD. Gently, gently! Be careful, you fool.
MISS CUBBIDGE. (*gasps*) Is she . . . is she . . . dead?
BLUEBEARD. (*listens to SYBIL's heart and genital through stethoscope*) No, she is not dead. She's just resting, waiting for new life to come.

(*There is the sound of thunder and flashes of lightning. MRS. MAGGOT and SHEEMISH light candles, incense. There are science-fiction lighting effects.*)

RODNEY. It is a new life or a monster you are creating, Baron Prevert?
BLUEBEARD. The word is "pervert." I believe in this monster as you call it.
RODNEY. So, this is the House of Pain.
BLUEBEARD. How do you know when you unlock any door in life that you are not entering a House of Pain? I have thought nothing of pain. Years of studying nature have made me as remorseless as nature itself. All we feel is pain. But we must take risks if we are to progress.
RODNEY. How could you? How could you?
BLUEBEARD. Do you know what it feels like to be God, Parker?
RODNEY. (*spits in BLUEBEARD's face*) I spit in your face.

BLUEBEARD 47

BLUEBEARD. Do you think that the envenomed spittle of 500 little gentlemen of your mark, piled one on top of the other, could succeed in so much as slobbering the tips of my august toes? (*He turns his back on RODNEY and, with the assistance of SHEEMISH, begins unwinding the bandages that envelop SYBIL. When she is completely nude except for her fuck-me pumps, the genital begins to move*)

BLUEBEARD. Look, it's moving. It's alive. It's moving. It's alive! It's alive! (*SYBIL moves like the bride of Frankenstein, with stiff, jerking movements of the head and neck. First she looks at SHEEMISH and screams with horror, then she looks at BLUEBEARD and screams with horror, then she looks at her new genital and growls with displeasure.*)

SCENE 10
LAMIA, RODNEY, SYBIL, MRS. MAGGOT, SHEEMISH, MISS CUBBIDGE, BLUEBEARD

LAMIA. (*enters and crawls over toward SYBIL with catlike stealth and examines the third genital*) Now no man will ever want her! Rodney is mine. (*She leaps toward RODNEY. BLUEBEARD fires on her and she falls.*)

BLUEBEARD. I told you never to come to this side of the island again.

SHEEMISH. (*kneeling over LAMIA's body*) You killed the woman I love.

BLUEBEARD. (*Going to her also, feeling her pulse*) Woman—I wouldn't say she was a woman. She was a leopard, a wild cat. I couldn't make my leopard love me.

SHEEMISH. You killed the woman I love. Now you

must die. (*He moves toward BLUEBEARD threateningly.*)

BLUEBEARD. (*backing away*) No, Sheemish, no! Remember the House of Pain!

SHEEMISH. I no longer fear pain. My heart is broken. (*He seizes BLUEBEARD by the throat.*)

RODNEY. (*looking at SYBIL's genital*) No man will ever want her?

MISS CUBBIDGE. (*to MRS. MAGGOT*) What are you doing with the lapis lazuli locket? Sybil's mother gave it to her the night she died when the terrible fire . . . Sybil's real mother had a strawberry birth mark on her left knee cap.

RODNEY. I need never be jealous again!

MISS CUBBIDGE. Margaret, Margaret Maggot? Maggie! (*SHEEMISH releases BLUEBEARD in amazement.*)

MRS. MAGGOT. The fire? Margaret Maggot? It's all coming back to me. I am Maggie Maggot. (*turning to BLUEBEARD*) What have you suffered for that child that you dare to tear her from me without pity? Sybil is my daughter. I am her real mother. If you give me back my child, I shall live for her alone. I shall know how to tame my nature to be worthy of her always. My heart will not open itself to anyone but her. (*on her knees*) My whole life will be too brief to prove to her my tenderness, my love, my devotion.

BLUEBEARD. (*kicking her over*) I detest cheap sentiment.

MISS CUBBIDGE. This exploits women!

MRS. MAGGOT. Women want an answer! (*They seize BLUEBEARD, tie ropes to his wrists and stretch him across stage. LAMIA rises and begins strangling him slowly.*)

BLUEBEARD. Lamia! I thought you were dead.

LAMIA. My dear, didn't you know? A cat has nine lives.

SYBIL. (*The monster speaks haltingly.*) Stop . . . in . . . the . . . name . . . of love. The human heart . . . who knows to what perversions it may not turn, when its taste is guided by aesthetics? (*The women drop the rope. LAMIA releases BLUEBEARD. The sound of the ship's foghorn is heard off stage.*)

SHEEMISH. (*looking out the spy hole*) The *Lady Vain*! The *Lady Vain*! The *Lady Vain* has weathered the storm!

MISS CUBBIDGE. (*to BLUEBEARD*) I am leaving this moment. Tomorrow I shall be far away. I shall have forgotten everything that happened yesterday. It's enough to say that I will tell nobody, nobody. If, as I hope, you regret the words that escaped you, write to me and I shall despond at once. I leave without rancor wishing you the best, in spite of all. I am carrying your child. Would that your son will be your good angel. (*hands him the key to the laboratory*) Adieu! Come, Margaret, Sybil, Rodney. We must return to normalcy. (*They exit. There is the sound of a foghorn.*)

SCENE 11
BLUEBEARD, LAMIA, SHEEMISH

BLUEBEARD. (*in a rage; Shaking his fists at the heavens*) I curse everything that you have given. I curse the day on which I was born. I curse the day on which I shall die. I curse the whole of my life. I fling it all back at your cruel face, senseless fate! (*laughing*) With my curses I conquer you. What else can you do to me? With my last breath I will shout in your asinine ears: Be accursed, be accursed! Be forever accursed! I'm a failure, Sheemish, I'm a failure.

SHEEMISH. But, Master, you have heart, you have talent.

BLUEBEARD. Heart! Talent! These are nothing, my boy. Mediocrity is the true gift of the gods. (*exit*)

SCENE 12
SHEEMISH, LAMIA

SHEEMISH. Come, let us do the best we can, to change the opinion of this unhappy man. (*exit with LAMIA*)

Prop List

Act I

Preset on Table
A skull.
A rack containing test tubes.
A large book of Bluebeard's formulas.
Scene 1
A broom.
A feather duster.
A test tube that Mrs. Maggot carries onstage concealed under her dress.
Scene 3
Bluebeard carries on a pistol.
Scene 6
A whip.
Scene 7
Rodney, Sybil and Miss Cubbidge bring on luggage.
Scene 11
Sheemish and Mrs. Maggot bring on a dinner table (must be strong enough to support a lot of weight), chairs, place settings, and platters of food.
Mrs. Maggot carries an ear trumpet with an ear on the end of it.
Scene 12
Sybil wears a lapis lazuli locke throughout the play.

Act II

Scene 1
Rodney carries a lace hanky.

Scene 3
A key.
Scene 7
Leopard-print fan.
Sheemish carries a flower.
Scene 8
A key on a chain.
Scene 14
Sybil carries a candle.

Act III

Preset
Bluebeard's book of formulas and apparatus.
Scene 2
A bottle of blood.
A paintbrush.
Mrs. Maggot brings on a snake.
Scene 5
Mrs. Maggot brings on the locket.
The switched test tube.
Scene 9
Candles.
Incense.
Bluebeard wears a stethoscope.

Costume Plot

Sheemish: Distressed blue suit. White shirt. Black boots.

Mrs. Maggot: White mob cap edged in pink. White blouse with green polka dots.

Lamia the Leopard Woman: Wearing more leopard than the costume designer thought advisable.

Bluebeard: (Act I, Scenes 3–10) Khaki safari suit with zebra trim. Black shoes.
(Act I, Scenes 12–13) Fez, purple velvet jacket with dragons on shoulders. White bejeweled harem pants. Curled shoes.
(Act II, Scenes 2–4, 8–9, 11) Full-length wine-red lounging robe. Wine-red silk pajamas.
(Act II, Scenes 15–16) White lab coat, shirt, pants, shoes.
(Act III, except Scene 6) Same as Act II, Scenes 15–16.
(Act III, Scene 6) The lab coat is covered with blood.

Good Angel: Golden hair, wings, halo, etc.

Bad Angel: Dressed like the devil.

Sybil: (Act I, Scenes 7–8) Blue chiffon and ecru lace blouse, trimmed in red and blue ribbon. Blue satin skirt trimmed in red and blue ribbon. Black fur cape. Black shoes.
(Act I, Scenes 12–13) White lace dress trimmed with red. A red ribbon belt. Red shoes.
(Act II, Scenes 1–2) Two-piece peach silk and chiffon dress embroidered with pearls.
(Act II, Scenes 8–12, 14) White flowing nightgown.
(Act III, except Scene 6) Same as Act II, Scenes 8–12, 14.
(Act III, Scene 6) Wrapped in bandages like a mummy.

Rodney: (Act I, Scenes 7–9) White shirt. Brown tie. Brown herringbone tweed suit. Brown coat. Brown shoes.

(Act I, Scenes 12–13) Black formal dinner attire.

(Act II, Scenes 1, 5) Dark brown and white houndstooth jacket. Tan pants. Brown shoes. White shirt. Green print tie.

(Act II, Scenes 16–17; Act III) A tattered version of the costume worn in Act II, Scene 1.

Miss Cubbidge: (Act I, Scenes 7–8) Green wool suit. Beige blouse. Dark green coat trimmed in brown velvet. Brown shoes.

(Act I, Scenes 12–13) A maroon dress trimmed in black lace and black velvet. Black shoes.

(Act II, Scenes 3, 9–12; Act III) Black jacket. Gray skirt with black trim underwear. Black merry widow. Black petticoat. Black garters. Black stockings. Black shoes.

Hecate: Black sheath. Purple and silver cape. Blue goatee.

Other Publications for Your Interest

THE ROCKY HORROR SHOW
(MUSICAL)
Book, music and lyrics by RICHARD O'BRIEN

7 men, 3 women. Various ints. and exts.

At last! The original stage version of the cult movie that has been a "12 O'clock high " for thousands of enthusiastic movie-goers. Live, on stage, see Dr. Frank N. Furter match wits (?) with the innocent young newlyweds! Thrill to the delightfully trashy rock and roll music! "It isn't a play, it isn't a musical, it isn't a rock concert...It's a sort of glitter, rock, horror, comedy, tranvestite circus...And if you love—say, 'Sound of Music'—you will probably hate it."—WABC-TV. "*The Rocky Horror Show* is a sicko-wacko-weirdo rock concert. It keeps trying to blow your mind with loud music and perverted sexuality, but it is so simple-minded, and so completely silly, that it ends up being a lot of fun. It may get a cult following, even though there is no nudity."—NBC.
(#20049)

(Restricted. When available, Terms quoted on application—Music available on rental.) Posters Available

VAMPIRE LESBIANS OF SODOM
(ADVENTUROUS GROUPS.) FARCE
By CHARLES BUSCH

6 men, 2 women. Unit set

This truly bizarre entertainment, cut right out of the *Rocky Horror* genre, is about vamps, has nothing to do with lesbians and takes the audience from ancient Sodom to the Hollywood of the twenties, ending up somehow in present day Las Vegas. "Costumes flashier than pinball machines, outrageous lines, awful puns, sinister innocence, harmless depravity—it's all here. One can imagine a cult forming."—NY Times. "Bizarre and wonderful...If you think Boy George is a gender-bender, well, like Jolson said, you ain't seen nothing yet! Forget your genders, come on, get happy."—Broadway Mag. Published with *Sleeping Beauty.* or *Coma*. (Royalty, $50-$40.) (#24006)

ACT I & II DROP

CUTOUT WINDOW

ACT III DROP - HOUSE OF PAIN

SL LEG

CHAISE LOUNGE (ACT II)

PORTAL

CHAIR (ACT I)
TABLE (ACT I)

SR LEG

SCENE DESIGN
"BLUEBEARD"